RELIGION FOR TODAY

Christianity for today

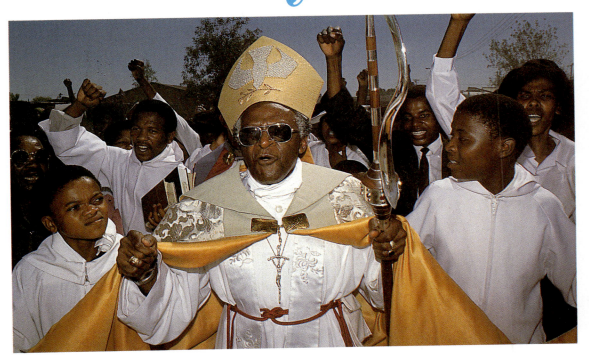

Carrie Mercier

OXFORD

About the series

We live in a world where there are people of many different religions. In many of our towns and cities Buddhists, Christians and Jews live alongside Muslims, Hindus and Sikhs. If you travel abroad you will soon experience whole countries that have been shaped by religion.

We all have different ways of looking at things. It could be said that we all see the world through our own "spectacles". These spectacles are made up of our beliefs, opinions, attitudes and values. What is important to you, might not be important to me.

Religious people see the world through their spectacles, which affects the way they see and live in the world. We can't understand someone else's worldview unless we look through their spectacles. The *Religion for Today* series helps you to do this by giving you the skills and knowledge to understand people with beliefs different from your own.

In learning about another religion you will also be given the chance to think about your own life. So you will not only learn about the religions you study, you will also learn from the religions.

Chris Wright, Series Editor

About this book

This book celebrates the variety of practices and the diversity of traditions within the Christian faith, but it also emphasises the unity of the Christian community. All Christians accept Jesus as Lord and try to follow his example and his teachings. All Christians are working towards a common goal – to bring about God's Kingdom on earth. Christian symbols and rituals may look different from the outside, but they express common values and a sense of belonging to a tradition that continues.

Whether we are from the Christian faith or not, we know what it feels like to sing songs, to say sorry, to hope for a better future, or to stand up for what we think is right. This book builds on the common ground between Christians and non-Christians. It looks at many of the everyday feelings and experiences that we are all familiar with in order to throw light on the Christian experience of life.

Carrie Mercier

Practical hints

- Words you may not be familiar with are explained in the text. You can also check their meaning in the Glossary at the back of this book (page 62).

- We learn about Jesus from the Bible. The first part of the Christian Bible is called the Old Testament; the second part is called the New Testament. There are a number of references in this book to the Bible. A reference will look like this:

    Matthew 5:17.

In this reference:

Matthew is the name of the book. You will find a list of the books of the Bible at the beginning of the Bible.

5 is the number of the chapter. In the Bible the chapter numbers are printed large.

17 is the number of the verse. The verse numbers are printed much smaller.

- Dates are given as CE (in the Common Era) or BCE (Before the Common Era). Jesus was born in about 6 BCE.

CONTENTS

	About the series	2
	About this book	2
1	What is a Christian?	4
2	Belonging	6
3	Following	8
4	Listening	10
5	Reading	12
6	Talking about God	14
7	Seeing	16
8	Praying	18
9	Asking for help	20
10	Singing	22
11	Eating together	24
12	Giving thanks	26
13	Serving others	28
14	Hoping: Advent	30
15	Going to Bethlehem: Christmas	32
16	Forgiving	34
17	Getting wet	36
18	Making promises	38
19	Grieving and remembering: Lent	40
20	Rejoicing: Easter	42
21	Receiving the Spirit: Pentecost	44
22	Learning from others	46
23	Journeying	48
24	Living and loving	50
25	Finding a path in life	52
26	Fighting	54
27	Being caretakers	56
28	Facing death	58
29	Celebrating life	60
	Glossary	62
	Index	63

ONE

WHAT IS A CHRISTIAN?

In this unit you will discuss what makes a Christian and consider whether it depends on what they do or what they believe.

  1 *What do you associate with Christianity – any particular symbols, books, people, places, customs, ceremonies and festivals? Brainstorm your ideas on paper with a partner. Draw a circle around just one of the things you have written down – the one that you think the most important. Compare your ideas.*

There are millions of Christians across the globe. Christians today come from many different countries and cultures. This makes Christianity a very exciting religion to study as there is such variety in the practice and expression of the faith. Despite all the differences, most Christians believe that they belong to one big family.

Christians today belong to a faith that goes back 2000 years. This helps to explain why there are many different Christian traditions. A religion is a bit like a snowball. As it rolls through history it draws into itself layers of the past. However, the centre, on which everything else has built up, remains the same.

At the heart of the Christian faith is a person, Jesus Christ. Christians believe that Jesus Christ was God on earth. The word "Christian" comes from the title "Christ". Christians see Jesus as their Lord and King. In other words, they try to make Christ the most important influence in their lives.

2 *What are the most important influences in your life – parents? friends? television? What rules your life? Discuss your thoughts with a partner. Share your thoughts in class.*

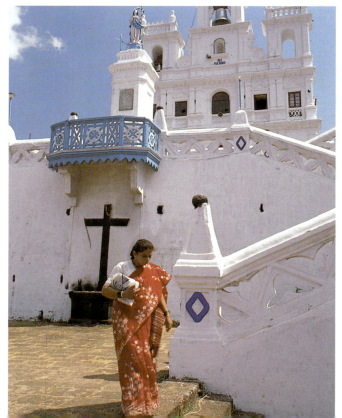

4

3 Which of these statements do you think describes a Christian?

(a) Someone who goes to church on Sunday.
(b) Someone who is good and gives to charity.
(c) A person who believes in God.
(d) A man or woman who follows the teachings of the Bible.
(e) A person who accepts Jesus as his or her Lord.
(f) Someone who has been baptised.
(g) One who loves God and loves his or her neighbour.
(h) A person who keeps the Ten Commandments.
(i) Someone who wears a cross.

Put your choices in order of importance. Compare your list with those of a partner. Do your definitions of a Christian emphasise what they believe or what they do? Write a paragraph explaining your definition of a Christian.

4 Look at the photos. Which of these people do you think are Christians and which do you think are not? Write your answer giving your reasons. Discuss your answers.
(You will find the answer on page 62.)

5 Ask two people you know who are Christians to say what it is that makes each of them a Christian. Share your class findings and write up a few notes on what you have found out.

5

TWO
Belonging

In this unit you will learn how Christianity is a family of different groups. You will think about what it means to belong to a family or group.

1 *What communities, groups and families do you belong to? List them. Decide on one of these groups and say in what ways your belonging is expressed, e.g. experiences shared, feelings, rules, symbols, leaders, relationships. Write down your answers and then discuss them with a partner.*

Christians belong to the Church. The word "church" has a number of meanings. It can mean the universal Church — that is the community of Christians everywhere. Within this worldwide community there are smaller communities also called churches. For example, there is the Roman Catholic Church, the Orthodox Churches and then there are Protestant churches.

The word "church" is a bit like the word "family". When you draw a large family tree it is made up of lots of smaller families with grandparents, parents and children, aunts, uncles and all their children. The Christian Church has a large family tree made up of many families. Some of these families are mentioned here, but there are others too.

2 *Look at the photographs. Take each in turn and make a note of clues that tell you the people belong to a community.*

> ❝ I belong to the Greek Orthodox Church. The Orthodox Church could be called the grandmother of the Christian family. The way we worship goes back to the worship of the earliest Christian communities. ❞
> [Peter, 15]

> ❝ I belong to the Roman Catholic Church. Like all Christians we follow Jesus. Jesus called St Peter to lead his followers after he had gone. Today the Pope is leader of the Roman Catholic Church. He is the successor of St Peter. ❞
> [Matthew, 14]

> ❝ I'm an Anglican. Like other Protestant Churches we do not accept the Pope as the head of the Church. But we do have bishops, and in some ways our worship is similar to that of the Roman Catholic Church. ❞
> [Alison, 13]

> ❝ I am a Baptist. Baptist churches are independent. In other words, we choose our own leaders and decide how we run our services. Our beliefs are based on the teachings and example of Christ. Jesus taught his disciples to baptise believers. We've kept this practice of baptism in our church. ❞
> [Sarah, 14]

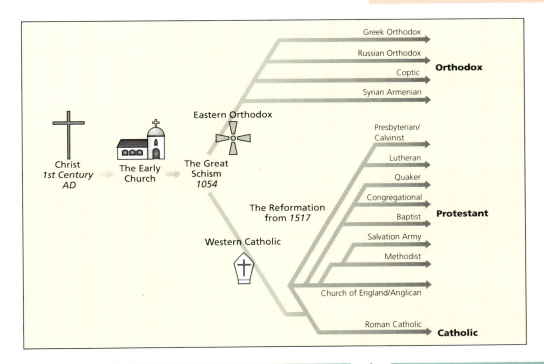

This is the family tree of the Christian Church.
- *With a partner discuss which family names you recognise or know.*
- *Make a set of six questions to go with this diagram to exchange with another pair, e.g. which churches are parents to the Salvation Army? When was the big split between the Orthodox and Roman Catholic tradition?*

3 *Write four headings: Orthodox Churches, The Roman Catholic Church, The Church of England, and Independent or Free Churches. Under each heading write down at least three things you have learnt about each of these. Use the family tree and the quotations to help you.*

4 *Imagine you are selling the idea of Christianity as one family. Design a poster to show that Christians of different Churches hold many beliefs in common, e.g. worshipping one God, accepting Jesus as Lord, having the Bible as their holy book.*

THREE

Following

In this unit you will think about what it means to follow someone. You will also look at how Christians follow Christ.

Most Christians are following the faith of their family. Their religion is as much a part of them as their language and their culture. Others choose to become Christians and have no such family tradition. Whatever the path by which they entered the faith, Christians look to Jesus Christ as their Lord and follow him.

Jesus was a Jew who lived in Palestine 2000 years ago. He was a famous teacher and thousands came to hear him. In his teaching, Jesus proclaimed that God was like a loving parent. Everyone, he said, was a child of God and we must therefore love one another.

Many men and women who heard Jesus teach were moved by his words and the love and compassion he showed for ordinary people. The first people to follow Jesus were called his disciples.

1 *Look at the leaders illustrated on this page. Write a sentence on each to say who they are and why people follow them. Add examples of two other leaders you can think of.*

2 *Write four or five sentences to explain what you think it means for a Christian to follow Jesus. Say how Christians today are like the very first disciples. Use the painting on the page opposite and the quotations to help you.*

3 *Look at the painting by the poor peasants of Solentiname. Design a picture that the poorest people from this country might paint to tell the story of Jesus calling the disciples as if they were people like themselves.*

4 *Following someone can sometimes be a mistake. Suggest three occasions when this might be true. Are there ways of testing whether you are mistaken about whom to follow? Suggest three ways. Write answers to these questions. Discuss them in class.*

Like the first disciples, Christians today feel called to follow Jesus. In other words, Christians are not following a set of dry doctrines but a person.

> ❝ When I became a Christian I felt as if I had been found. I felt as if Christ had come and found me and called me personally to follow him. ❞
> [Angela, 15]

> ❝ I try to follow Jesus in my daily life. I try to think what he would want me to do in every situation. Sometimes I turn my back on him but then I do things I regret later. ❞
> [Gavin, 16]

> ❝ If you are a Christian your life cannot be driven by your own ambition or selfish goals. You have to let Jesus lead the way. ❞
> [Derek, 17]

> ❝ Following Jesus means trying to be like him. It means spending time in prayer, being ready to forgive, finding time for other people and putting their needs first. ❞
> [Samantha, 16]

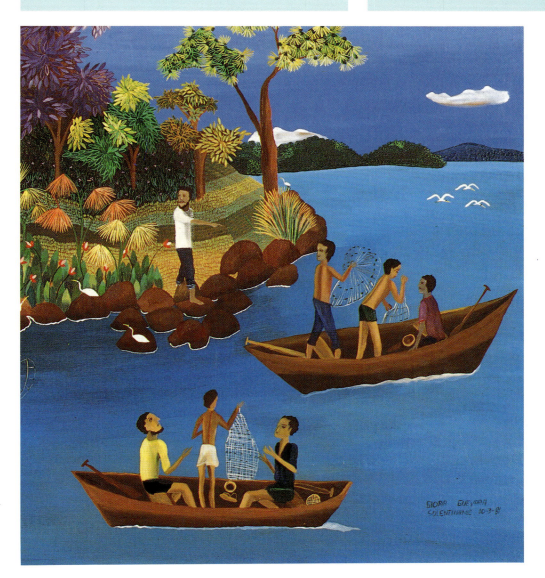

This is a picture of Jesus calling his first followers. (Read Mark 1:16–20.) It is a painting by the peasants of Solentiname, some of the very poorest workers in Nicaragua in Central America. These people felt called to follow Jesus.

- *Describe carefully what you see in the picture and say why you think the poor people of Nicaragua painted this story the way they did.*

FOUR
LISTENING

In this unit you will think about how you listen, and learn how listening is important to Christians.

 Design a poster or collage illustrating the way in which people are constantly bombarded with "voices" demanding their attention – for example, advertisements and politics. Do you think that sometimes people just stop listening? Write a few sentences about this problem today.

There are different kinds of listening. We can be passive listeners – absorbing information but not responding. On the other hand we can be active listeners, open to new ideas and ready to respond.

 Describe two occasions when you were listening – one where you were passive and one where you were an active listener. Compare your experiences with those of a partner.

The story of Christianity began with people listening to Jesus. Some recognised the truth of his message and followed him. Others felt uncomfortable about what he was saying. They looked for ways to get rid of him so that they would not have to listen to him. In the end they had him executed.

Listening plays an important part in the life of the Christian. In many churches Christians listen to the words of the Bible and hear the teachings of Jesus. In some churches the worshippers listen to a sermon. This may be an opportunity for the priest or minister to explain the teachings of the faith or to challenge people listening in church or to offer them words of encouragement or comfort.

When members of the Society of Friends (Quakers) meet they sit still and listen. With this sort of listening there need be no sound that you can hear. "We wait for God to tell us what to do. If he wants to speak, we believe he will also give us the words... It is not only those who speak in meeting who help others. Our feelings can be shared without any words being spoken." (*The Quaker Way*)

Listening can be the first step in becoming a Christian. Some Christian preachers try to reach out to non-believers to tell them about the love of God and the life of Jesus. Thousands flock year after year to hear the famous evangelist Billy Graham, whose photo is on the next page. Many who have listened to him preaching have come to accept Jesus as their Lord and Saviour.

3 Look at the photos. Read the text again. Decide which listening activity matches each photo. Write a set of notes on the importance of listening for Christians today.

4 Christians are told to listen to what God wants them to do. Read the story Jesus told about the house built on the rock (Luke 6:47–49). What does this story say about how Christians should listen? Write a sermon that a Christian minister or priest might give based on the teachings of this famous story.

This is a picture of Jesus teaching. Answer these questions in writing:
(a) What does the picture show?
(b) What is the artist saying about Jesus?
(c) Who do you think this picture is for?
(d) What is it telling Christians to do?

FIVE
Reading

In this unit you will think about how important reading is to you and find out why reading is important to many Christians.

1. *Make a list of the different kinds of things you read every day, e.g. notices, adverts, books, papers, comics, your own writing and other literature. Put them in order to show which influences you the most. Write a few sentences on the list you have drawn up and explain what it says about your reading habits.*

The Bible is being read from a special stand in church called a lectern.

"The Bible contains the word of God. It is our holy book. When the Gospel is read in church we stand as a mark of respect."
[Francis, 14]

2. *Do you know someone who reads the Bible? When do they read it? How often? Where do they read it? Do they read it out aloud or in silence? Is it a special copy of the Bible they use? Write your answers and compare your notes with a partner.*

3. *Look at the photos and quotations. How can you tell that the Bible is a special book for Christians? Explain in writing, describing what you see and giving your reasons.*

4. *Read the story about Jesus in Luke 4:16–21. Jesus was Jewish so he was reading from the Jewish Scriptures. Write a few sentences about the story and what it tells Christians about (a) Jesus' work and (b) the way in which he understood the Scriptures.*

The Bible has two parts. The first part is called the Old Testament. It contains the sacred scriptures of the Jews. These writings Jesus would have known and loved. Christians believe that these scriptures tell of God's work in the world before the arrival of Jesus Christ.

The second part of the Bible is the New Testament. This includes the four Gospels. The word "Gospel" means good news. These four books tell people about the Good News of Jesus Christ. The New Testament also contains the story of the first Christians and the writings of the early Church.

In many churches the Bible is the main influence in all activities. The sermon, hymns and prayers are all based on its teachings and readings from the scripture are given centre stage in the service. In these churches the pulpit is the main focus rather than the altar.

Some Christians believe that every word of the Bible is to be taken at face value as word-for-word literally true. Others see that there are different kinds of writing in the Bible: poetry, drama, stories and letters as well as history. Read the passage below from Luke's Gospel. Some Christians take this as an account of what actually happened. Others say the story describes the experience of faith – those who trust in Christ can find calm and peace in the face of fear, trouble or anxiety:

> " One day Jesus got into a boat with his disciples and said to them, "Let us go across to the other side of the lake." So they started out. As they were sailing, Jesus fell asleep. Suddenly a strong wind blew down on the lake, and the boat began to fill with water, so that they were all in great danger. The disciples went to Jesus and woke him up, saying, "Master, Master! We are about to die!"
>
> Jesus got up and gave an order to the wind and the stormy water; they died down, and there was a great calm. Then he said to the disciples, "Where is your faith?"
>
> But they were amazed and afraid, and said to one another, "Who is this man? He gives orders to the winds and waves, and they obey him!" "
> [Luke 8:22–25]

Some copies of the Bible are very beautifully decorated and treasured by the community.

" I have Bible reading notes. They give a passage to read each day and notes to explain the meaning. Reading the Bible helps me to understand the life and teaching of Jesus and I find that the stories make me think about the way I live my life. "
[Sandra, 12]

" Mostly I read passages from the New Testament. I like the Gospels best. Sometimes I read parts of the Old Testament. I also read the writings of other Christians; their thoughts and experiences can help me understand my faith. "
[George, 15]

5 Tell the story of the calming of the storm in your own words and say what you think it means.

6 Look up Luke 6:27–36. Write your own version of what Jesus says. Give three reasons to explain why you think a Christian should know these teachings and read them often. Say how it should influence their lives.

SIX

Talking about God

In this unit you will be talking about your ideas of God and learning about the Christian idea of God.

 Write your answers to the following questions and then compare your responses with those of others.

(a) When you were younger what ideas did you have about God?
(b) How have your beliefs changed?
(c) Do you believe that God exists?

In the Bible God is described in many ways, for example he is Creator, King, Judge and Shepherd. Jesus spoke of God as a Father. Many Christians today say we should talk about God as Mother too.

Some Christians may say it is not easy to talk about God. They say God is invisible so how can we describe him at all? To add to the problem, Christians believe that God is neither male nor female so any human image of God creates problems. In fact there is a tradition in Christian thinking which attempts to define God by saying what God is not: God is not made. God is not seen. God is not limited by time or space.

Young people discussing their beliefs about God.

Woman will play God

A woman has been chosen to play God in the York Mystery Plays this June. Not everyone is happy though.

 What six words would you use to describe (a) a good father and (b) a good mother? Do you think any of these words have been used to describe God? Discuss your answers in small groups. Debate whether Mother is as good an image for God as Father.
Write up the different points of view in this debate.

Write down six more negative statements (like the ones above) that Christians might use to say that God is beyond definition. In your own words explain why some Christians talk about God in this way. Say whether you think this is a helpful way for Christians to talk about God.

Christians talk about God as a "Father". He is the Creator and Father of all humankind. Christians also talk about God the "Son". This is the person Jesus Christ. He is the "Saviour" who came to earth to help men and women find their way back to God. Christians also believe in God the "Holy Spirit" who gives life to the people of God. The Holy Spirit is the power and presence of God in the world, working through Christians everywhere. The Christian idea of God as Father, Son and Holy Spirit is called the Trinity. Jo, aged 12, said: "Just as a person can be a teacher, a sister and a mother so God has different ways of making himself known to people. God is Father, Son and Holy Spirit. We call God Three in One."

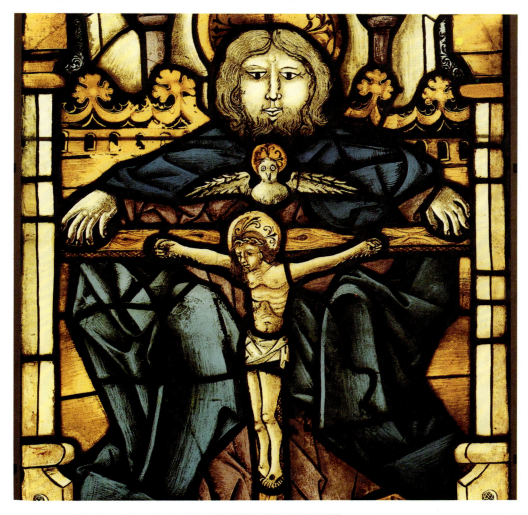

This stained glass window presents an image of the Trinity. Can you find the Father, the Son, and the Holy Spirit?

4 *The Trinity is sometimes shown in a symbol, e.g. the three leaves on a shamrock or the three sides of a triangle. Design a diagram to explain the Christian idea of God as three in one. Explain the meaning of your diagram and say how it helps to illustrate the Christian teaching on the Trinity.*

5 *Words such as "goodness", "truth", "love" are often used to describe the nature of God. Write down six more words used in this way. Write down what all these words mean in everyday life. Do Christians use the words in the same way when they are talking about God?*

15

SEVEN

Seeing

In this unit you will think about how we see and yet sometimes don't see. You will also learn how looking and seeing are important in the Christian response to life.

In what ways does this photograph illustrate people being blind?
- *Describe your own examples of people failing to see anything beyond their own needs, or their own narrow point of view, or show your examples in cartoon form.*

Christians are meant to live with their eyes open. Some people are unable to see because they are suffering from a physical disability. Others are blind because they do not want to see. You could say that they go around with their eyes closed. Jesus confronted those who were blind and failed to see the truth about themselves.

Jesus made people see. He cured the blind and gave them their sight. He made people see in another way too. He helped them to recognise God's work in the world around them. He made them look beyond outward appearances to see the goodness and love in the lives of ordinary people. Read this story from Luke's Gospel:

> " Jesus looked round and saw rich men dropping their gifts in the temple treasury, and he also saw a very poor widow dropping in two little copper coins. He said, "I tell you that this poor widow put in more than all the others. For the others offered their gifts from what they had to spare of their riches; but she, poor as she is, gave all she had to live on. "
> [Luke 21:1–4]

> **1** Read Luke 18:35–43 and Luke 6:39–42. What are the two kinds of blindness described here? Write one of these as a story for children in words and pictures, that Christians might use for Sunday school.

> **2** Read Luke 21:1–4. What did Jesus see that others failed to see at the temple? Think of examples of goodness that go unnoticed or that people are blind to today. Write a "good news" front page for a newspaper to uncover the goodness and love in the world that goes unnoticed.

Images and symbols can help us to see. Some pictures and posters can make us look and see things in a new light. This is why images, symbols and pictures are important in some Christian traditions.

> **3** Which posters, images or TV programmes have helped you to see important truths about life and the world? Describe one image, poster or programme that has made you stop and think about things more deeply. Say what it meant to you.

Some Christians find that icons and pictures help them to see.

❝ I find the icon of Christ as judge is very powerful. Some Christians say pictures of God are wrong as people will worship the picture rather than God. But I find they are helpful in telling us truths about God and Jesus. ❞
[Marga, 15]

❝ We have pictures in our church and I have some on my wall at home. The one I like best is Jesus as the good shepherd. ❞
[Jeanne, 16]

> **4** Do you know someone who keeps a photo in their wallet, or a poster of a special person, or a picture of someone they love? Describe three examples of pictures, photos or posters that are very important to people. Say why they are important.

> **5** Look at the paintings above. Write a few sentences on each (a) to describe the picture, (b) to say what you think the artist is saying about Christ, (c) to say why Christians find these pictures helpful.

EIGHT

Praying

In this unit you will think about the practice of prayer and learn how prayer is important to Christians.

1 Which of the following do you think might be true of prayer?
Prayer is ...

a time for being alone
a community activity
listening to God
being calm, quiet, at peace
talking with God
talking to yourself
like meditation
a way of recharging the batteries
allowing time for your inner life

Discuss your views in pairs and then in class.

Jesus prayed. Sometimes he went off on his own to pray in the wilderness. On other occasions he went to the synagogue and the Temple in Jerusalem to pray. Jesus taught his followers how to pray. He said:

> When you pray, say this: Father: May your holy name be honoured; may your Kingdom come. Give us day by day the food we need. Forgive us our sins, for we forgive everyone who does us wrong. And do not bring us to hard testing.
> [Luke 11:2–4]

2 Look at the photos in this unit. In writing, describe what you see in each photo. Say what you think these people are doing. Explain how you can tell that what they are doing is important to them.

Christians find different things helpful when they pray. Many Christians close their eyes. In some churches Christians kneel for prayer. In Orthodox churches they stand as a sign of respect. They believe that prayer is standing before God.

"People think that when Christians pray we just get a nice cosy feeling inside. There is nothing very cosy about standing before your Maker."
[Natalie, 15]

> **3** What do you think Natalie means by "standing before your Maker"? Express your view of what you think she means in a drawing, a painting, a poem or a script for a play.

> **4** Write down the reasons you think Christians might give for the following things they do when they pray:
>
> (a) closing their eyes
> (b) kneeling
> (c) standing.
>
> Compare your answers in class. Write up your answer fully after the discussion.

> **5** Christians find teachings on prayer in the Bible. Read Matthew 6:5–13, Luke 18:9–14 and Mark 11:15–17. Discuss the meaning of these teachings. In your own words write down the main message of each. Say why you think Christians might take these teachings seriously.

This woman is using a rosary to pray. She moves a bead each time she says a prayer.

When Christians pray together they may recite well-known prayers or follow a prayer book. Sometimes they use no words at all and pray in silence. On other occasions prayers are sung or chanted.

> "Christians can pray anywhere and at any time. I find it is important to set aside some time for prayer every day. I say my prayers last thing at night when it is quiet."
>
> [Marianne, 15]

> "When my grandma prays she goes to church and lights a candle. It makes it special. At home she uses rosary beads to pray – to count the different prayers as she says them."
>
> [Michelle, 14]

> **6** Design a leaflet to raise awareness of the different ways of praying in Christian practice and to show its importance. Illustrate the variety of ways in which people pray. Use symbols, pictures, prayers and the words of Jesus in your leaflet.

NINE
SKING FOR HELP

In this unit you will think about those who support and help you in times of need. Christians sometimes pray for help – this kind of prayer is called intercession.

 Answer the following questions in writing:

(a) Who do you look to for support in times of trouble?
(b) What kind of support do they give?
(c) Describe one occasion when you were really grateful for someone's help or support.

Being a Christian does not make problems of life go away. What do you think the Christians in this church in India ask for in their prayers? Do you think their prayers would be different from the prayers of people in churches in the UK?

Jesus warned his followers that there would be hard times ahead. Being a Christian does not make the problems of life go away. However, Christians believe Jesus promised to be with them in their struggle in life. Christians find that their faith gives them courage and strength in times of trouble.

Christians are told that their prayers will be answered: "And so I say to you; Ask, and you will receive; seek, and you will find; knock, and the door will be opened to you. For everyone who asks will receive, and he who seeks will find, and the door will be opened to anyone who knocks." (Luke 11:9–10)

" O Lord, we beseech thee to deliver us from the fear of the unknown future; from fear of failure; from fear of poverty; from fear of bereavement; from fear of loneliness; from fear of sickness and pain; from fear of age; and from fear of death.

Help us, O Father, by thy grace to love and fear thee only, fill our hearts with cheerful courage and loving trust in thee; through our Lord and Master Jesus Christ. Amen "

[Francis Akanu Ibiam, Nigeria]

 This prayer could have been quite different – it could have asked for an escape route and an easy life. Rewrite the prayer in these terms. Why do you think that Francis Akanu Ibiam did not offer this kind of prayer? Write your answer and say how his prayer is different from the one you wrote.

Christians believe that God answers prayer. However, they know this may be in unexpected ways:

> He prayed for strength that he might achieve;
> He was made weak that he might obey.
> He prayed for wealth that he might do greater things;
> He was given infirmity that he might do better things.
> He prayed for riches that he might be happy;
> He was given poverty that he might be wise.
> He prayed for power that he might have the praise of men;
> He was given weakness that he might feel the need of God.
> He prayed for all things that he might enjoy life;
> He was given life that he might enjoy all things.
> He received nothing that he asked for – all that he hoped for;
> His prayer was answered – he was most blessed.

 3 *What is the message of this story? Write the story in comic-strip pictures and words or write your own version of the story.*

> Every day I pray for peace, for an end to war and for everyone to have enough to eat. But I can't see that this prayer will ever be answered in my lifetime. Perhaps one day.

[Philip, 12]

> If sometimes our poor people have had to die of starvation, it is not because God didn't care for them, but because you and I didn't give.

[Mother Teresa of Calcutta]

 4 *Are Mother Teresa's words an answer to Philip who feels his prayer is not answered? How might Philip's prayers be answered? Write a conversation on prayer between two people – one a Christian who believes that prayer is answered and someone who claims that prayer is not answered.*

 5 *Read this prayer from Melanesia. Design a poster to illustrate this prayer or a prayer of your own:*

O Jesus
Be the canoe that holds me up in the sea of life;
Be the rudder that keeps me in the straight road;
Be the outrigger that supports me in times of temptation.
Let your Spirit be my sail that carries me through each day.
Keep my body strong, so I can paddle steadfastly on in the voyage of life.
Amen

A Christian Aid worker brings food to Rwanda in Africa. Christians pray for help and help others. Is this worker an answer to prayer?

TEN

Singing

In this unit you will think about why people sing and use music to express themselves and you will learn how Christians express their beliefs and their feelings in music.

> **1** Look at the photos. How can you tell that these people are expressing something that means a lot to them? Write down your observations and compare them with those of a partner.

> **2** Why do people sing? When do you sing? What are most songs about? Which of the songs you know express feelings? Which feelings? Write your answers to these questions and discuss them in class.

One of the things that many Christians enjoy doing is singing. In the Bible Christians are told to "sing psalms and hymns and sacred songs; sing to God with thanksgiving in your hearts". (Colossians 3:16) Christians today sing hymns of praise when they gather for worship.

A choir singing a Christmas carol in Salisbury Cathedral.

> " All glory be to God on high,
>   And to the earth be peace;
> Good-will henceforth from heaven to men
> Begin and never cease. "

> **3** Look at the words of the carol. What does it tell you about what Christians believe? Write the words for a song that reflects the things that you believe and feel about life, about truth or about the world.

Not all Christian songs express praise and thanksgiving. Some songs are an expression of outrage against injustice. Others call for freedom and express hope for a better future:

" We shall overcome
    We shall overcome
We shall overcome some day.
Deep in my heart
I do believe
We shall overcome some day. "

For many Christians the Gospel story reflects their own experience in life. In times of hardship they look at Jesus' life and suffering and feel that God has shared in their pain. Music is a way in which they can express their feelings:

" Nobody knows the trouble I see,
    Nobody knows but Jesus;
Nobody knows the trouble I see,
Glory Hallelujah!
Sometimes I'm up, sometimes I'm down,
O yes Lord! Sometimes I'm almost to the
    ground;
Nobody knows the trouble I see,
Nobody knows but Jesus;
Nobody knows the trouble I see,
Glory Hallelujah! "

Christians at a Jesus Rally in Durban, South Africa, in 1994.

"Take That" performing in 1993.

4 Do you know a song that expresses sadness, loss, grief or just feeling low? What words are used to describe the feelings? What sounds, what colours, what images and symbols express these emotions? Discuss these questions and write or draw your answers. Design a cover for a CD of Christian songs expressing these feelings.

5 Describe three occasions when people sing together as an expression of their unity and sense of belonging. Say how this might help us to understand why Christians enjoy singing together. Describe a time when Christians sing together.

6 Listen to examples of sacred music. When you listen write down the thoughts and feelings that come to mind. Compare your thoughts with a friend and discuss how the music affected you.

ELEVEN

Eating Together

In this unit you will explore why people like to eat together, and think about why it is good to share meals. You will find out that sharing food is important to Christians too.

1 Why do people choose to get together to eat? Make a list of important shared meals that you know. Compare your list with that of a partner. Discuss the meaning of the occasion in each case.

2 Organise a shared meal for your class. Remember to take into account the different diets. Make the meal special in some way, e.g. speeches, music or candles. Write an account of the meal and what it was like for the class to eat together.

Christians eat together. This was something Jesus taught his followers to do. In many Christian homes the family meal is a time to remember God's goodness. A prayer of thanksgiving is said before the meal and the food is accepted as a gift from God. In some churches community meals are organised. At harvest time the meal may be combined with a thanksgiving service at the church.

These Christians are enjoying a meal together in a community called "The Open Door" in the Cotswolds.

66 In our church we hold a shared meal of just bread and water. In this way we remember that many people in the world do not have enough to eat. The money that would have been spent on a full meal is then given to a charity. 99
[Alan, 12]

66 At our Salvation Army headquarters we run soup kitchens to provide meals for the homeless. Jesus commanded us to feed the hungry – and the meals are also a way of bringing fellowship and love into the lives of people who are very lonely. 99
[Martin, 15]

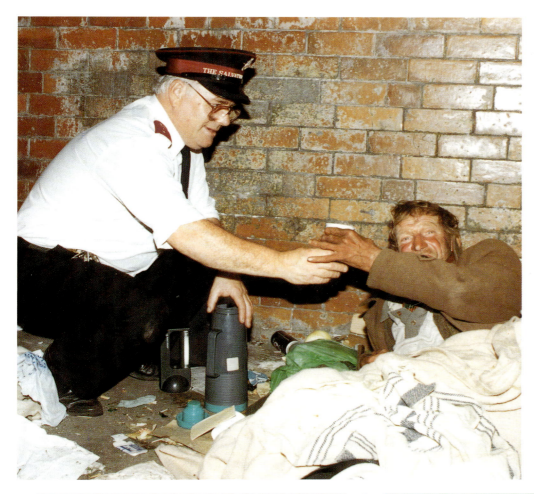

A Salvation Army officer dispenses soup to a homeless man in Glasgow.

3 Some say that there are two kinds of hunger – one is the hunger of the stomach, the other is the hunger of the heart or soul. Draw or describe two menus – one that would fill the empty stomach and one to feed the other kind of hunger.

4 Research among the very poor and homeless in New York showed that they did not want another fast-food service for their soup kitchens. They wanted a sit-down meal not a take-away. Why do you think this is? Discuss your ideas in class.

Fourteen-year-old Chris said that in the Society of Friends they try to make every meal a special occasion. "When we share food we remember that Jesus taught us to live in friendship with one another. We give thanks for the fellowship and the food."

5 If you wanted people to live in friendship with one another how would you try to organise it? Could you bring it about with laws and rules? Write your answer and discuss your ideas in class.

6 Jesus taught people to eat together and to share food and to give thanks. Do you think these three things are still important today? Give your answer in writing, explaining your reasons. Design a poster for a home or community kitchen which reminds Christians of these important teachings.

TWELVE

IVING THANKS

In this unit you will think about what it means to say thank you and you will learn about a special meal that Christians share in which they remember and give thanks for Jesus.

1 *What are the different ways in which people say thank you? e.g. sending flowers. Why is it important to say thank you? What does it feel like when a friend forgets to thank you for something? Write your answers to these questions. Share your thoughts with a partner.*

In many churches, Christians share a meal of bread together. There are many names for this event. In some churches it is called the Eucharist, which means thanksgiving. In other traditions it is called "Holy Communion", or "Holy Liturgy", or "Mass". Christians also call it the Breaking of Bread, or the Lord's Supper. Whatever the name given to this special meal, Christians are remembering the last meal Jesus shared with his friends and giving thanks for his love.

Soon after the Last Supper Jesus was arrested. He was then tried on false charges and taken away to be executed. He died hanging on a cross. Read this account of the Last Supper:

> While they were eating, Jesus took a piece of bread, gave a prayer of thanks, broke it, and gave it to his disciples. "Take and eat it," he said; "this is my body."
>
> Then he took a cup, gave thanks to God, and gave it to them. "Drink it, all of you," he said; "this is my blood, which seals God's covenant, my blood poured out for many for the forgiveness of sins. I tell you, I will never again drink this wine until the day I drink the new wine with you in my Father's Kingdom."
>
> Then they sang a hymn and went out to the Mount of Olives.

[Matthew 26:26–30]

Members of a Baptist community share the Breaking of Bread.

2 *Prepare a version of the story of the Last Supper in words, symbols, quotations, photos from newspapers and pictures.*

3 *In what ways do people get ready for a special meal or party? Christians believe that God is concerned with what is in a person's heart not what he or she is wearing. How might a Christian prepare for the Lord's Supper? Write your answer explaining your suggestions carefully.*

At the Eucharist, Christians ask God to forgive them all they have done wrong before they accept the bread and wine. This prayer is said in some churches: "Almighty and most merciful Father, we have sinned against thee and against our neighbours in thought and word and deed and in what we have left undone ... forgive us all that is past and grant that we may serve you in newness of life."

This communion is taking place in a Roman Catholic church, where it is called "Mass".

❝ We call the bread and wine the sacraments. Sacraments have been called "earthly gifts which carry heavenly blessings". ❞
[Frances, 17]

❝ In our church the Eucharist has two parts. The first is the Ministry of the Word when we listen to the teachings of the Bible. The second is the Ministry of the Sacrament when we receive the bread and wine. ❞
[Carolyn, 13]

❝ When I receive the bread and wine I think of Jesus at the Last Supper when he knew he was going to die. I feel grateful that he left us this special way to remember him – it's a way to feel close to him and to others too. ❞
[Linda, 14]

❝ At Communion we thank God for the love of Jesus and accept the gift of forgiveness. You feel like you have been given a fresh start and can try again. ❞
[Robert, 13]

4 *Remembrance, sorrow, forgiveness, joy, new beginnings, friendship, thanksgiving – in a design for a church window show how each of these is important in the story and celebration of the Last Supper. If you prefer, answer in the form of a poem or prayer.*

5 *Look at a written service for the Breaking of Bread or Holy Communion from the Alternative Service Book of the Anglican Church or from the prayer book from another Church. Find prayers that reflect the themes of remembrance, sorrow, repentance, forgiveness, joy, new beginnings and thanksgiving.*

THIRTEEN

ERVING OTHERS

In this unit you will be thinking about what it means to serve others. You will also learn how Christians are meant to understand service.

One of the things that Christians are asked to do is to serve others. Often people talk about "helping" others, but Jesus talked about *serving* others and this is different. It is not about someone rich or powerful helping someone poor and helpless at arm's length. It is about forgetting oneself, being close to to others and putting the needs of the other person first.

Jesus told his followers to love one another. At the Last Supper he set an example of love and service to others by washing the feet of his disciples. In some churches Christians wash one another's feet. This is the story in John's Gospel:

1 In pairs discuss examples of two types of help – one where the help is given at arm's length and one which is an example of true service. Write down your examples and explain the difference between them.

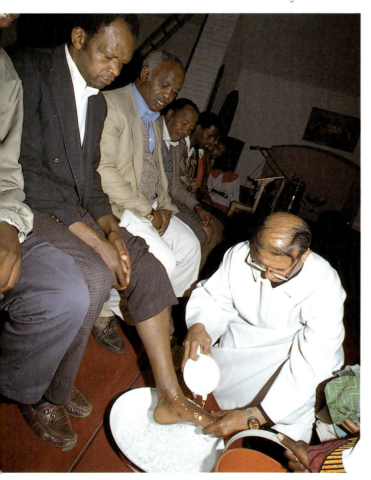

In some churches they have followed the example given by Jesus in a practice called "the washing of the saints' feet". The service here is happening in Johannesburg, South Africa.

66 So Jesus rose from the table, took off his outer garment, and tied a towel round his waist. Then he poured some water into a basin and began to wash the disciples' feet and dry them with the towel round his waist. He came to Simon Peter, who said to him, "Are you going to wash my feet, Lord?"

Jesus answered him, "You do not understand now what I am doing, but you will understand later."

Peter declared, "Never at any time will you wash my feet!"

"If I do not wash your feet," Jesus answered, "you will no longer be my disciple."

Simon Peter answered, "Lord, do not wash only feet, then! Wash my hands and head, too!" 99

[John 13:4–9]

66 When we wash each other's feet we are following Jesus' example. We are also learning a very difficult lesson. We are learning humility – to forget ourselves. 99

[Jackie, 13]

2 *Why do you think that washing one another's feet offers a good model of service? Serving others is not always easy. Think of examples when it could be difficult. Write down three examples. With a partner discuss what you have written.*

Martin, aged 14, said that Jesus' example of service tells Christians about how Jesus saw his work on earth. "Jesus said that the Son of Man came not to be served but to serve. He also said that the people who love and serve others are the most important people in God's eyes."

3 *Service can sometimes hurt. Read Matthew 20:20–28. Tell a story in which giving or serving others hurts.*

4 *Draw a diagram to show who is at the top and who is at the bottom in our society. Draw another diagram to show how this would be different in God's society – if the rules were set according to the teaching of Jesus.*

Look at this picture, then read Matthew 25:31–46.
▸ Tell your own version of Jesus' teaching in words, pictures or both.

❝ Providing transport for people who cannot get around, keeping the church clean, making coffee for the Senior Citizens Club – these are all ways in which we can offer service. ❞
[Sandy, 16]

❝ When we are working with the homeless, the lonely and the rejected people in our society, people think that we are the givers. But in fact we are the ones who receive. ❞
[Rachel, 18]

Christians believe that in serving others they are serving Jesus. Mother Teresa said: "Because we cannot see Christ we cannot express our love to him; but our neighbours we can always see, and we can do for them what, if we saw him, we would like to do for Christ."

5 *The idea of service has gone out of fashion. Imagine you are an advertising expert. You are asked to bring the word "service" back into fashion. Design a poster/advert to raise awareness of the true meaning of service.*

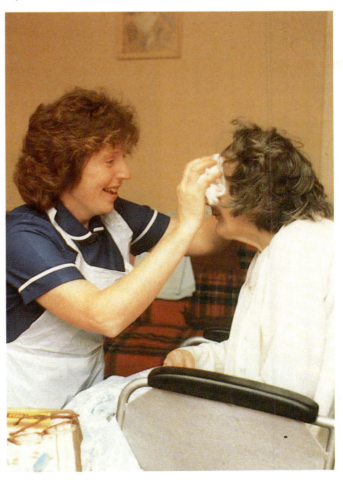

FOURTEEN

Hoping: Advent

In this unit you will be sharing ideas about how people have hopes for the future. You will learn about the Christian hope for the future.

Jesus taught his followers to long for and work for God's kingdom (Luke 12:35–40). Seventeen-year-old Frances said: "When the world learns to live in peace and people love and respect each other, then we can say that Christ reigns on earth. We hope one day this will come about."

> **1** What hopes do people have for the future? What safety measures do they take to provide for themselves, their homes and families? Discuss your ideas with a partner.

People who collect for organisations such as Christian Aid hope to work with God to make the world a better place.

"The kingdom most people strive for is based on saving up wealth and looking after your own interests. God's kingdom is about sharing, and about looking after the needs of others."
[Stephanie, 13]

Advent is a time of great hope for Christians. It is the period leading up to Christmas. At Christmas Christians celebrate the coming of Christ. The word Advent means "coming". Advent is the beginning of the Christian year.

> **2** Do you have any longings that are not just about your personal well-being but about your hopes for the future of the world? Write your answer in the form of a letter to a newspaper.

> **3** Why are new beginnings times of hope? Write down three examples of new beginnings in the life of a person or the life of a country. With each example say what hopes people have at these times of new beginnings.

At Advent Christians often remember the words of John the Baptist. Mark, who is 16, said: "John prepared the way for Jesus. His words remind us that we need to prepare for the coming of Jesus in our hearts and in our lives."

> **4** Read Mark 1:1–12. What is the message given here in the words of John the Baptist? Write your answer and say why you think these teachings are important and relevant for Christians today.

> **5** Look up two passages from the Old Testament: Isaiah 40:1–11 and 42:1–9. What hopes for the future are expressed here? Write a song or hymn for Advent based on these readings; or write a poem which expresses the hopes and longings similar to those expressed in these passages.

"We call Jesus 'the Light of the World'. For me, light is a symbol of hope. In our church a candle is lit each Sunday of Advent to mark the approach of Christ's coming at Christmas."
[Sally, 14]

Chrissy Cole has just lit a candle in the Church of the Nativity in Bethlehem.

> **6** In what ways is the world a dark place? Collect pictures and newspaper cuttings to make a collage on the theme of light and hope coming into a dark world.

FIFTEEN

Going to Bethlehem: Christmas

In this unit you will think about what it is like to travel in your mind. You will also learn how Christians travel to Bethlehem through the stories, carols and images of Christmas.

This crib scene is from Venezuela in South America.

At Christmas Christians are called to go to Bethlehem. Of course not everyone can pack up and go. Christians travel in their hearts and minds, in their thoughts and prayers. They listen to the stories about the birth of Jesus and sing carols that tell of God coming to earth. In many churches the figures from the story of the birth of Jesus are put in the Christmas crib. Thirteen-year-old Jane said: "In our church we have a crib. When we look at it we are reminded of the example of the shepherds and in our hearts and minds we go to Bethlehem and bow down and worship the Christchild with the shepherds."

1 *Do you ever travel in your mind? Where do you go? To a real place or an imagined one? To a holiday you remember? Write your answers to these questions. Compare your travels in class.*

2 *Read Luke 2:1–20. When Christians read this story they travel to another time and to another place. Write the story as if you had travelled in time and space – imagine you are suddenly in Bethlehem and see things for yourself.*

> Night of nights, the night of present night,
> which is not the present night
> but the night of Christmas Eve,
> Christmas Eve of olden time,
> when the holy Son was born,
> holy Son on His good earth.
>
> [A Romanian carol]

 3 What has happened to the sense of time in this carol? What does this say about Christmas? Find an example of a carol that takes you to Bethlehem. Write out two verses and explain what you believe their meaning is for Christians today.

Pictures of the Christmas story help believers in their journey to see the Christchild. They unfold the meaning of the story. The message of Christmas is that God became flesh and blood and lived on earth. Christians call this event the Incarnation.

Icons are different from other pictures. The unusual standpoint and perspective is a reminder that the truth being explained in the image is not of this world.

> At the centre of the icon the figure of Christ is shown as a tiny baby wrapped in swaddling clothes. He is the smallest figure in the icon. This tells us about Jesus' humanity. God has really entered the world as a child ... It also teaches us that the Incarnate Christ did not appear in his full glory – he emptied himself of that glory ... to become as men are. The cave where Mary has placed Christ in a manger is a dark hole, which already looks like a tomb. Christ has entered the darkness, sin and death of the world, and he too is capable of feeling our weaknesses and temptations. He too will taste death. His humanity is complete.
>
> [Orthodox Outlook]

4 Design a symbolic picture of one part of the Christmas story and explain the message you think it has for Christians today. Give a detailed explanation of the symbols in your picture.

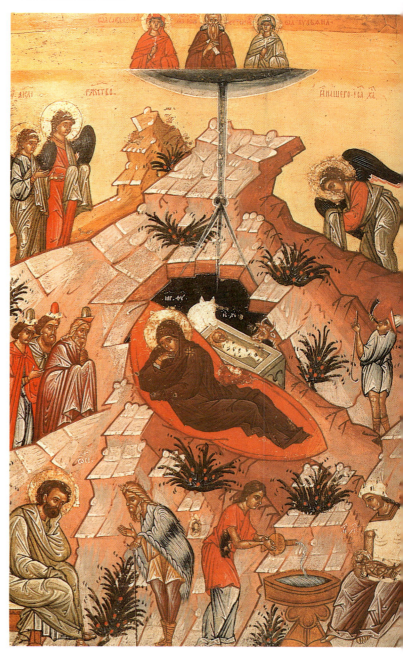

This Russian icon is about 400 years old. It shows Mary and Jesus inside the cave.

SIXTEEN

FORGIVING

Is it easy to forgive and forget? In this unit you will find out how Christians understand the meaning of forgiveness.

The hardest thing Jesus asked his followers to do was to be forgiving.

Jesus taught his followers that God forgives those who do wrong no matter how bad they have been or how great the sin. Fourteen-year-old Thomas says that "asking for God's forgiveness without the intention of doing better is meaningless. We must want to try again." Christians also believe that because God forgives them they should forgive others.

Christians find that feelings of shame and sadness at having disappointed God are not easy to live with. Asking God's forgiveness for the things they have done wrong is a part of their worship. Saying sorry and asking for forgiveness in this way is called repentance. Sixteen-year-old Craig said: "You cannot be forgiven unless you want to be forgiven. When you have done something wrong you cannot enjoy being close to God until you say sorry. Being forgiven is like being healed."

1 When someone has hurt you or done you wrong what is your reaction? Do you want to hurt them back? Do you want to make them suffer? Why do people feel this way? Discuss these questions in groups and then in class.

2 Read Matthew 18:23–35. Write a summary of the story. Say what you think the message of the story is for Christians. Explain how you could retell the story to make it meaningful for non-believers too.

Forgiveness works!

When I discovered that my best friend had been talking about me behind my back I felt hurt and angry. I thought we could never be friends again. I was sad and lonely but I could not accept what she had done. Then she came and said that she was really sorry and she asked what she could do to help things get better between us. Once she said she was sorry I found I could forgive her – it was OK to forgive her. It felt good to put it behind us and now we are the best of mates.

In Belfast thousands gather for a peace rally. Is the first step to peace forgiveness? Discuss this question.

3 Can you think of any time when you have decided to forgive someone or they have decided to forgive you? What happened next?

Jesus' followers were shocked to see him forgive the people they saw as too sinful to have contact with. On one occasion Jesus was having dinner with a wealthy and highly respectable man called Simon. During the meal a woman who had a bad reputation, and was known to be a sinner, came into the room and anointed Jesus' feet with perfume:

> Then Jesus turned to the woman and said to Simon, "Do you see this woman? I came into your home, and you gave me no water for my feet, but she has washed my feet with her tears and dried them with her hair. You did not welcome me with a kiss, but she has not stopped kissing my feet since I came. You provided no olive-oil for my head, but she has covered my feet with perfume. I tell you, then, the great love she has shown proves that her many sins have been forgiven. But whoever has been forgiven little shows only a little love."
>
> Then Jesus said to the woman, "Your sins are forgiven."
>
> [Luke 7:44–48]

This picture was painted by Tintoretto, who lived in Venice in the 16th century.

 Read the whole of the story in Luke 7:36–50 then write the story as a play, filling in detail in the conversation. You could use a modern setting and example.

 In which of the following situations would forgiveness be very hard? Write your answers and discuss them in class.
- A parent has a child killed by a drunken driver.
- A boy finds his sister has left his bike out and it has been stolen.
- A woman loses her husband in a terrorist attack.
- A girl finds her best friend has been dating her boyfriend.
- A teenager hears his friend saying bad things behind his back.
- A husband finds his wife has been unfaithful.
- A people that had suffered under an evil ruling class is given the chance to live with their rulers in peace and freedom.
- A nation remembering the cruelty of its enemy in the last war.

Jesus asked his followers to forgive even when it is hard and the hurt is very deep. Christians believe that forgiveness can begin the healing process in situations where bitterness and mistrust have built up.

 Write a story about saying sorry and being forgiven – a story that Christian parents might use to explain forgiveness to their young children. You may find the story Jesus told of the lost son helpful in thinking about your ideas (read Luke 15:11–32).

SEVENTEEN

Getting wet

In this unit you will think about what it means to make a new beginning. You will learn about baptism, which is a mark of a new beginning and an important symbol for Christians.

1 What new beginnings have you had in your life? Draw a map of your life so far and mark on it the different new beginnings. What new beginnings lie ahead of you in life? Put them on your map too. Compare your life map with that of a partner.

Jesus told his disciples to go and baptise people. Today Christians are still baptised. Baptism is a mark of repentance and a new beginning. For many Christians it indicates a change from a life which is self-centred to one which is God-centred. Baptism is also a mark of becoming a member of the Church, it is a sign of belonging.

In some Churches babies are brought for baptism soon after they are born. This is called infant baptism, or christening.

At the christening service the parents promise to help the child grow up to love and trust in God. Godparents are chosen for the child. They are often friends or relatives of the family. Bridget, aged 14, said: "At our church the parents and godparents promise to bring the child up to fight against evil and to follow Christ. They are given a candle. This is to show that we have passed from darkness to light."

2 Look at the pictures. What are the essential features of baptism? What do these pictures have in common? Discuss the main features of the baptisms that pupils in your class have seen or attended.

Not all Churches baptise children. In the Baptist Church they wait until a person is old enough to make the promises and commitments for themselves before they baptise them.

> ❝ Going under the water and coming up again is symbolic. We are dying to a life that is self-centred and we are born again into a new life that is Christ-centred. ❞
> [Keith, 15]

> ❝ I got baptised because I wanted to make a new start and let Jesus rule my life. I was really nervous. But once I was standing in the water my fear left me. Our minister said, "I baptise you in the name of the Father, the Son and the Holy Spirit," and then supported me as I went under. ❞
> [Nicky, 16]

3 Write an interview with someone who has been baptised in which they describe the ceremony and explain its meaning.

4 Write down all the powers and properties of water. Look at how water is used in advertisements and in other ways as a symbol. What does it represent? Say what you think the symbol of water means.

5 Jesus is sometimes called the "Living Water". What do you think this means? Design an invitation card for a believer's baptism using the symbol of water to express the meaning of the service.

6 Baptism is very important for Christians. There are arguments about what is the right time to get baptised. Prepare a debate on the question of adult versus child baptism.

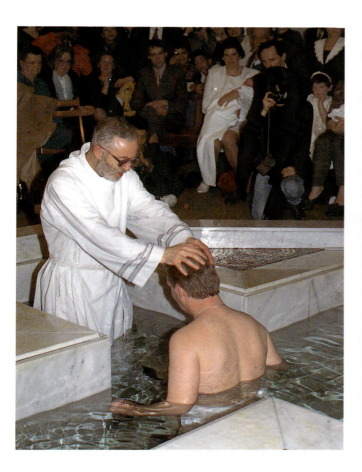

EIGHTEEN

MAKING PROMISES

In this unit you will discuss what it means to keep a promise and make a commitment and learn about some of the promises that Christians make.

1. Write down the promises that people might make in the following situations: (a) two countries ending a war between them, (b) someone going away having to leave their girlfriend or boyfriend for a long time, (c) two friends who have made up after falling out, (d) a parent to a child who is going away to college, (e) a couple getting married. Compare your ideas in class.

2. What do you now take responsibility for that your parents or guardians took responsibility for when you were much younger? Write down some examples. Say how and at what stage the responsibility changed hands. Compare your experiences in class.

The majority of Christians are baptised as children. As they grow up many Christians want to make their own personal commitment to Christ. Some Churches have a special service called "confirmation". It is an opportunity for Christians to make the promises that were made for them by their parents and godparents when they were baptised as children.

In the Anglican Church Christians have to answer the following questions:

Do you turn to Christ?

Do you repent of your sins?

Do you renounce evil?

In both the Roman Catholic and Anglican confirmation services a bishop confirms the candidates. Laying his hand on each one he says: "Confirm O Lord your servant with your Holy Spirit."

"Before we got confirmed we had classes taken by our minister. He helped us understand the teachings of the Church and we discussed the Bible, prayer and Holy Communion. We were able to ask questions and talk to others getting confirmed."
[Sophie, 14]

This is a Roman Catholic confirmation in England.

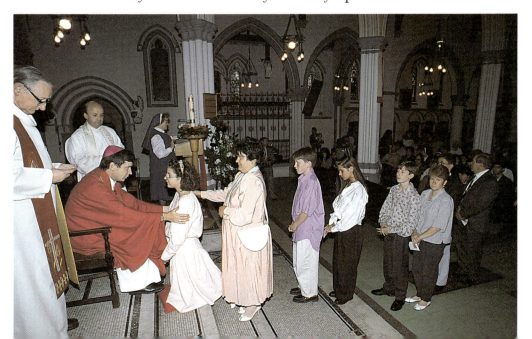

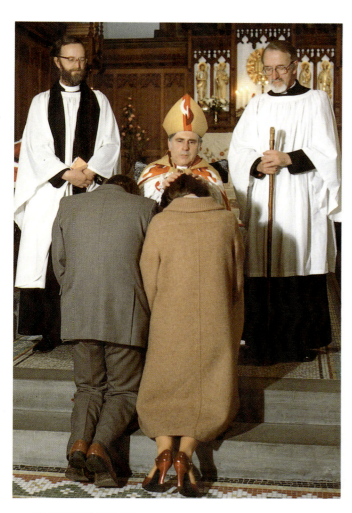

A confirmation in an Anglican church. The bishop is wearing a special hat called a "mitre". His chaplain holds his crook, a stick which shows that a bishop is a "shepherd" to his people.

In the Anglican Church, being confirmed allows the Christian to receive Communion for the first time and it marks the occasion when they take on full membership of the Church.

❝ My confirmation was a very special occasion for me. I was making an important statement about what I believed and how I wanted to lead my life. That day I received the bread and wine for the first time. ❞
[Clair, 15]

❝ Confirmation is about making a commitment to something I really believe in. It is about taking responsibility for my own faith. I'm ready to take my religion seriously now. ❞
[Victoria, 15]

> **3** Look at the photographs. Use these and the quotations to help you make a church leaflet telling worshippers about confirmation and its meaning for Christians.

> **4** What do you hold really strong beliefs about? Animal rights? Nuclear power? Cycle paths? Capital punishment? How do you express your commitments? Discuss the different examples of commitment and belief in class.

> **5** In what ways do you think that a Christian might hope to live differently after confirmation? Discuss this question with a partner and then write your answer in the form of a letter from a newly confirmed teenager to his/her godparents.

> **6** People can get confirmed at any age. However, it is at about the age of 13 or 14 that most people get confirmed. Why do you think this is? Discuss your thoughts in class.

NINETEEN

RIEVING AND REMEMBERING: LENT

In this unit you will consider how people express sadness, grief and sorrow. You will learn how Christians observe a time of mourning and remember the last days in the life of Jesus.

 How do you behave when you feel really sad? How do you show your feelings? How do other people express sadness and grief? Write your answers.

Sometimes life is bewildering. One minute there seems to be such promise and hope. Then, suddenly, everything goes wrong and there is confusion, despair or death. This must have been how things seemed to the disciples when Jesus was arrested, tried on false charges and executed.

Every year Christians remember the suffering and death of Jesus. This time of remembering is called Lent. It begins on Ash Wednesday. Mark, aged 13, said: "In our church we have a special service on Ash Wednesday. We say sorry to God for all we have done wrong. The priest puts a smear of ashes on our foreheads as a sign of sorrow and repentance."

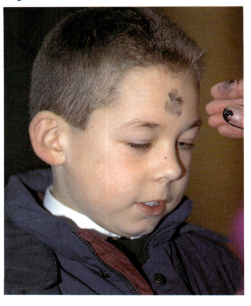

- *Why do you think that ashes are the symbol chosen by Christians to express feelings of sadness and repentance?*
- *What do you associate with ashes?*
- *What symbols do you think are appropriate for expressing grief and repentance?*

Answer these questions in writing, illustrating them if you wish.

Just as someone who is grieving has no interest in pleasures and distractions, so many Christians give up luxuries during Lent. Lent is a time of prayer and for some Christians a time of fasting.

 Read about how Jesus fasted in Luke 4:1–13. Have there been times when you have had to go without something you like? When was this? What was it like? What did you learn from the experience? Write your answers.

 Read Mark 14:10–15:47. Tell this story as a summary for a church newsletter from the vicar to the congregation.

Lent ends on Good Friday. This is a day of mourning when Christians remember the suffering and death of Jesus and listen to the story of the cross.

> Good Friday's a terribly sad day. The decorations in the church are removed and it feels very solemn.
>
> [Tessa, 13]

> We believe that when Jesus died he was sharing in the suffering of the world. This was an act of supreme love and self-sacrifice. Now we know we are never alone; even in death we are not alone.
>
> [Karen, 16]

> In our church we follow the stations of the cross on Good Friday. The pictures remind us of the suffering and death of Jesus and as we go round we listen to readings and prayers.
>
> [Catherine, 13]

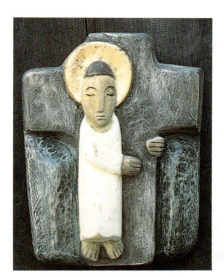

These pictures show just some of the stations of the cross. Can you match each one to an event in the Bible?

- *Design your own stations of the cross. Choose five points in the story of the cross or examples of suffering in the world today using collage or artwork.*
- *Write a few lines for each picture – e.g. verses from the Gospel or thoughts of your own.*

 The cross is the symbol for Christianity. Do you think that this is a good symbol? How does it capture the meaning of the faith? What does it tell you about the importance of the story of the cross for Christians? Discuss these questions in class.

TWENTY

Rejoicing: Easter

In this unit you will share ideas on how people express joy. You will also learn how to interpret the meaning of Easter for Christians.

1 *What event would make this day the happiest day of your life? How would you express your happiness? Write down six things that you would do. Compare your ideas in class.*

After Jesus' death on the cross, the disciples were filled with fear and despair. They had fixed all their hopes on this man yet he had been destroyed. There was no hope for the future, only darkness, fear and confusion.

Then something happened. The Gospels tell this story in different ways, but the message is the same. Jesus Christ was alive. He had overcome the powers of darkness and death.

2 *Look at the Easter stories in Matthew 28:1–9, Mark 16:1–8, Luke 24:13–35 and John 20:11–18. Draw up a list of the different emotions expressed in these stories. What do these feelings tell you about the message of Easter? Write your answer.*

At a church in London worshippers hold an Easter Vigil in the darkness just before daybreak.

Katrina, aged 15, finds it hard to express the emotions that she feels at Easter. "It is the happiness or joy of knowing that death is not the end of the story." Eleven-year-old Michael said: "Easter morning is very exciting. We wait and pray during the hours of darkness before the break of Easter Day. At dawn a large candle is lit and the priest says 'Christ is Risen' and we call out loud 'He is Risen indeed'."

In many churches Christians celebrate the Eucharist on Easter Day. They hear the story of the empty tomb and give thanks to God for the new life of Easter in hymns of praise.

" Lo! Jesus meets us, risen from the tomb;
  Lovingly He greets us, scatters fear and gloom;
Let the Church with gladness hymns of triumph sing,
For her Lord now liveth; death has lost its sting. "
[A hymn]

 3 Look at the photos. What are the ways in which Christians are expressing their joy and thanks? How do these compare with the ones you have listed in question 1?

Easter is a time of hope and renewal. Christians try to bring the feeling of new life into their everyday lives and homes. Fifteen-year-old Sandy said: "The children in our Sunday School build an Easter garden. This reminds us of the story of Mary meeting Christ in the garden. Because Easter is about new life the church is filled with spring flowers and the younger children get Easter eggs."

Desmond Tutu leads an Easter procession in South Africa.

 4 Prepare a class wall display to raise awareness about the meaning of Easter and the ways in which Christians express their joy.

 5 Is the power of life stronger than death? If death were the stronger, would all life have come to an end? Look at the words of Easter hymns. What are the beliefs expressed? Make up the words for a protest song against death to express the belief that life is stronger than death.

Easter cakes being blessed in a Russian cathedral.

"In our church families bring Paskha or Easter cakes to be blessed by the priest. After the service we eat hard-boiled eggs. When we break the shell we remember that Jesus broke open the grave and overcame death."
[Nicholas, 12]

TWENTY-ONE

RECEIVING THE SPIRIT: PENTECOST

In this unit you will discuss the meaning of the word "spirit" and how the word is used. You will learn about the gifts of the Spirit that Christians believe were given at Pentecost.

 Use the word "spirit" in three sentences to illustrate different meanings. Say what you think the word "spirit" means. People talk about God as Spirit. What do you think they mean? Write your answers then discuss your ideas in class.

Pentecost is the name of a Jewish festival that falls fifty days after Passover. According to the Christian Bible the disciples received the gift of the Holy Spirit on this day. Christians remember this event at the feast of Pentecost.

The story of the day of Pentecost is told in the fifth book of the New Testament, The Acts of the Apostles:

> " When the day of Pentecost came, all the believers were gathered together in one place. Suddenly there was a noise from the sky which sounded like a strong wind blowing, and it filled the whole house where they were sitting. Then they saw what looked like tongues of fire which spread out and touched each person there. They were all filled with the Holy Spirit and began to talk in other languages, as the Spirit enabled them to speak. "
> [Acts 2:1–4]

 Close your eyes for a minute. Picture what happened in Acts 2:1–4. What are the sounds, words, thoughts, images, symbols that come back to you? Write an account of the events of Pentecost in your own words.

This icon of the Pentecost comes from the Orthodox tradition.
▸ *Find the following symbolised in the icon: the disciples; the power of the Holy Spirit; the presence of God.*

In the icon the Holy Spirit is shown in flames of fire. What symbols were used to describe the Holy Spirit in the story of Pentecost? Look at how the Holy Spirit is pictured in the story of the baptism of Jesus in Luke 3:21–2. Design a church banner for Pentecost using the symbols of the Holy Spirit and quotations from the story.

Christians believe that all who follow Christ can receive the Holy Spirit. Some find the Holy Spirit in the silence of prayer. Others find its power in their church worship.

Pentecostalists hold a rally at Earl's Court in London.

66 Our church is a Pentecostal church. We believe that we can experience the Holy Spirit as people did at Pentecost. One way in which the Spirit works in us is through "speaking in tongues". This is the Spirit releasing you to praise God freely and fully in words and sounds of joy. 99

[Jemma, 15]

66 In the Bible it says that many people became believers and were baptised at Pentecost. In our church this is a popular time for baptism. 99

[Jesse, 12]

 If you wanted to give someone the six most precious gifts for life – ones that money cannot buy – what would you give them? Describe your gifts and say why you chose them.

The Bible tells Christians about the gifts of the Spirit. These include love, hope and faith.

 Find out about the gifts of the Spirit in 1 Corinthians 12:4–11 and 13:1–13. Which is the greatest of the gifts? Prepare a teaching aid with words and pictures that could be used to talk about the gifts of the Spirit with young children at Sunday School.

TWENTY-TWO

LEARNING FROM OTHERS

In this unit you will consider how people find it helpful to look back over the lives of those who have lived before them. You will discover how the lives of the saints are important to many Christians.

 1 *Do some members of your family have a photo album? How do they use this book of photos? What sort of thoughts, feelings and words arise when they look through the photo collection? Discuss your experiences in class.*

 2 *People, churches, schools and other communities are often named after saints – what examples can you discover close to you? Make a list and compare your collections. What does this tell you about the importance of saints in the United Kingdom?*

Christianity has a family album. Many Christians look back to the lives of the saints to learn from their example and to help them understand their own lives and their faith. The saints are Christian men and women whose lives show the power of faith, courage in the face of persecution and compassion for others.

In the Orthodox tradition a child is often named after a saint. Sometimes the child receives a small icon of the saint. In most Orthodox homes there is an icon corner. Eleven-year-old Catherine said: "At home we have an icon corner where we pray. My grandmother taught me how to cross myself before the icon. I do this first thing in the morning before saying the Lord's Prayer. I also have an icon of St Catherine on the wall in my room."

Many Christians like to have pictures of the saints. These ones are in a market in Mexico.

For many Roman Catholics, Mary the mother of Jesus is the most important of all the saints. They see her life as an example of perfect faith and obedience to the will of God. Maria, who is seventeen, said: "Mary has a special place in our Church and in our hearts. Just as God himself honoured Mary in choosing her to be the mother of his son so we honour Mary in our prayers, we light candles at her shrine and hold her with love and reverence in our thoughts."

> **3** Read the following stories about Mary the mother of Jesus – Luke 1:26–56, John 2:1–12 and 19:25–7. Write a summary of these stories. Say what these stories tell you about Mary.

> **4** Look at the two images of Mary. What kind of person have the artists tried to show? Write down the words that come to mind. Write a letter a Roman Catholic might write to a non-Catholic telling them about the importance of Mary.

This icon of the Virgin Mary and Jesus was painted about 600 years ago by Andrea Vanni.

Christians see the Church community as not only stretching across the world but also across the ages. In some churches, images and icons of the saints remind the worshipper that they are not alone in their efforts to lead a Christian life. Many before them have struggled to live lives pleasing to God.

> **5** What is your definition of a saint? Who are the saints of today? Can you suggest people who should become saints when they die? Share your ideas with a partner and discuss them in class.

> **6** Find out about the life of a Christian saint. Is there a special day to mark his or her importance? You could choose a saint associated with your local area. Make a class display on the different saints you have chosen.

TWENTY-THREE

Journeying

In this unit you will think about the way in which travelling brings knowledge and insight. You will also learn about religious journeys – pilgrimage, and its meaning for Christians today.

 Do you like journeys? What makes a journey interesting? Do you like to travel with others or alone? What can travel teach you? How can it be valuable? Write your answers. Share your experiences and ideas in class.

A journey can mean leaving behind familiar routines, seeing new places and meeting new people. In a sense there is an inner journey too. There may be a change of mood, a shift in attitude, a different outlook on life. It may mean being able to see things from a new perspective.

Write down the beliefs that are important to you, e.g. beliefs about human rights, animal rights, religion. Say how you could deepen your understanding about what you believe and why you believe in these things.

In pilgrimage there is an outward physical journey and an inner journey. The pilgrim is exploring the map of their own belief and faith as well as the holy places of their religion.

Many Christians travel to the Holy Land (in modern Israel) to see the places Jesus knew and to follow in his footsteps. Church buildings and shrines now mark the important sites in the life of Jesus.

66 In the garden of Gethsemane, where Jesus prayed in agony before his arrest, I just wanted to be still and just listen. I imagined Jesus praying. None of us spoke while we were there. The feelings were too deep for us to put into words. We were absorbed in thought and prayer. 99
[Christine, 21]

Pilgrims gather in Jerusalem to visit the site of the empty tomb and to listen to readings from the Bible.

" One of the best things was the friendship with others on the pilgrimage. We were brought together through the experience of the journey and through sharing our faith. We learned the meaning of a Christian community – the sense of being one. "

[Andrea, 19]

All over the world there are shrines and holy places dedicated to Christian saints. These have become places of pilgrimage.

Sometimes a pilgrimage can be a matter of taking a stand or making a protest. Christians have faced danger and hardship marching in protest against injustice or oppression.

 Find out about one Christian pilgrimage, e.g. Lourdes (in south-west France), Walsingham (in Norfolk). Prepare a short project on it. Indicate both the inward and the outward journey involved.

These Christians are protesting near the White House in America against the bombing of Iraq in 1993.

▶ *For which of the things you believe in would you be willing to march in the face of difficulty or danger? How could such a march be important? What purpose would it serve? Discuss your answers in class.*

 Life is sometimes described as a journey or a pilgrimage. Draw a life map. Indicate the main events in your life. Mark the points where you learnt about life and its meaning. Say where you think your learning points in life will come in the future.

 Make a board game called pilgrimage. Decide the destination, i.e. a place of pilgrimage such as the Holy Land. Ensure the journey includes tasks that will lead the pilgrim to a deeper understanding of their faith and religion. Use your knowledge and understanding of Christianity to help you do this.

TWENTY-FOUR
LIVING AND LOVING

In this unit you will consider what it means to love somebody and to be committed to someone. You will also look at some of the Christian teachings on love and marriage.

1 "Loving someone means …" Using speech bubbles, write three endings to this phrase. Share your ideas in class and add further speech bubbles to your page.

2 Read the words of St Paul in 1 Corinthians 13:4–11. Which of Paul's teachings on love would you want to include in your page on sayings about love? Write your answer. Say which of these teachings are important for people thinking of getting married. Give your reasons.

A Roman Catholic wedding in London.

In the Christian tradition marriage is a bond of love.

> Marriage is given by God. It is not to be entered upon or thought of lightly or selfishly; but responsibly and in the love of God. According to the teaching of Christ, marriage is the lifelong union in body, mind and spirit, of one man and one woman. It is his will that in marriage the love of man and woman should be fulfilled in the wholeness of their life together, in mutual companionship, helpfulness and care.
>
> *[The Methodist Service Book]*

> The Church of Christ understands marriage to be, in the will of God, the union of a man and a woman, for better, for worse, for richer, for poorer, in sickness and in health, to love and to cherish till parted by death.
>
> *[General Synod of the Church of England]*

Christians are taught to be faithful in marriage. Jesus taught, "You have heard that it was said, 'Do not commit adultery.' But now I tell you: anyone who looks at a woman and wants to possess her is guilty of committing adultery with her in his heart." (Matthew 5:27–28)

Mark's Gospel gives another of Jesus' teachings on marriage:

> Some Pharisees came to him and tried to trap him. "Tell us," they asked, "does our Law allow a man to divorce his wife?"
>
> Jesus answered with a question, "What law did Moses give you?"
>
> Their answer was, "Moses gave permission for a man to write a divorce notice and send his wife away."
>
> Jesus said to them, "Moses wrote this law for you because you are so hard to teach. But in the beginning, at the time of creation, 'God made them male and female,' as the scripture says. 'And for this reason a man will leave his father and mother and unite with his wife, and the two will become one.' So they are no longer two, but one. Man must not separate, then, what God has joined together."
>
> [Mark 10:2–9]

3 Using these words from the Bible and those of the churches, write a description and explanation of the nature and meaning of Christian marriage. Remember to mention God.

Before twenty-year-old Judith's wedding she and her partner went to see their minister. "He made sure that we had talked about the important questions that needed to be raised. He was very helpful and explained the meaning of the marriage ceremony."

4 What are some of the important questions a couple should talk about before they are joined for life? Write down your ideas. Look at the teachings of St Paul again (mentioned in question 2). Use his ideas and yours to write notes that a church minister might have for his or her talk with couples getting married.

5 Look again at Mark 10:2–9. In what ways are the lives that were once separate made one in marriage? Write your answer as a poem, or as a set of thoughts for reflection, or as a prayer that might be used in a marriage ceremony.

There are different sorts of Christian marriage ceremonies. In some Churches the marriage ceremony is conducted by the priest. There is a set service with prayers and readings from the Bible. In contrast, in the Society of Friends the marriage ceremony is simpler but no less serious. The couple each repeat promises in words which are 300 years old and which are recognised in law.

6 Design a wedding that says everything you would want in a marriage ceremony. Include prayers or poems, readings and symbols to illustrate the meaning and importance of the event.

In a Quaker marriage service held in 1979 the bride and groom face each other to make their promises.

TWENTY-FIVE

Finding a Path in Life

In this unit you will think about how you make decisions about your future. You will learn how some Christians try to let their faith influence the shape of their lives.

1. *What big decisions will you be making about your future in the next few years? How will you go about making these decisions? Write your answers and compare them with a partner.*

Christians believe that God has given them a variety of gifts and talents and these are not to be wasted.

2. *Draw a cartoon strip of someone coming to a major crossroads, having to decide which path to take in life. Show the different influences pointing them in different directions, e.g. making money, using skills, hoping for fame.*

❝ God has given me so much. I feel I should give something back. That's why I am going to work with deaf children. I enjoy working with children and get on well with them and I think it would be a way to put my gifts to good use. ❞

[Julia, 15]

GERMAN/ITALIAN/FRENCH DUTCH and ENGLISH
Speakers for
EUROPEAN TELEPHONE RESEARCH
Mother tongue preferred.
Temporary work providing research to companies (office hours only).
Training provided.

ACCOUNTS PERSONNEL
The successful applicants will be flexible, self-motivated, conscientious, possess common sense and have an eye for detail. Applicants should also be capable of working to tight deadlines.

PLUMBING/LEADWORK ESTIMATOR
An additional person is required to join the existing team in our well established plumbing division.

Meetings Executive
The ideal candidate will have a proven background in training development and promotion, as well as good administrative abilities.
Excellent communication skills and Windows computer literacy are prerequisites, as is the ability to work on own initiative to demanding targets.

HEALTH CARE ASSISTANT
We are looking for a person with a mature outlook and a flexible approach to caring to join our supportive, friendly team.

PART-TIME
SECRETARY / RECEPTIONIST
required to work on Wednesdays and Fridays, 10 hours weekly.
Good secretarial and receptionist skills.

3. *Describe ten gifts or talents people have, e.g. ability in maths or artistic skills. Say how each can shape a person's life and influence their choices. Would it be bad if these gifts were not used or wasted? Why?*

This is a story Jesus told (Matthew 25:14–30):

A man going on a journey gave his servants his money to look after:

Two of the servants invested the money; the other servant dug a hole and hid the money.

Then the third servant came in.

> **4** Read the whole story in Matthew's Gospel then write a summary or a modern version of this parable. What is this story saying? How might it influence Christians in the way they plan their lives? Write your answers as notes to explain the meaning of the parable.

Some Christians choose a path where the spiritual side of life comes first rather than material possessions, or personal ambition. There are Christian commmunities that are based on a life of poverty, simplicity and devotion to Christ. These are known as monasteries and convents.

❝ We go out to work in the wider community – as teachers or nurses. But in some monasteries and convents they give all their time to prayer. These communities are a reminder of the spiritual path in life. ❞

[Sister Mary, 36]

This nun in Tanzania is a part-time motor mechanic.

> **5** Which of the following might develop the spiritual side of life: shopping; watching TV; reading religious books or scriptures; watching the sunset; walking in the hills; listening to quiet music; visiting someone who is sick or lonely; rushing about being busy; reflecting on the meaning of things; sharing food; making money? Explain your choices and suggest other activities. Discuss ways in which people who are not religious can keep a place for the spiritual side to life.

TWENTY-SIX

Fighting

Christians are encouraged to fight. In this unit you will find out what they might fight against.

 What are the different ways in which you can fight? What do you battle with? What things do you struggle or fight to overcome in yourself – laziness, fear? Discuss these questions with a partner then share your ideas in class.

In the Anglican baptism service the minister says to the worshippers: "Fight valiantly under the banner of Christ." Every Christian is involved in the battle against evil. Sometimes the enemy is inside. Greed, envy, pride, selfishness, anger — all these are things that the Christian must struggle to overcome.

Look at the words of this hymn. What do they tell you about the way in which Christians view life? How does it compare with your view of life? Is it a race or a struggle? Is there anything you think you should be fighting against in life?

> Fight the good fight with all thy might,
> Christ is thy strength and Christ thy right;
> Lay hold on life, and it shall be
> Thy joy and crown eternally.
>
> Run the straight race through God's good grace,
> Lift up thine eyes, and seek his face;
> Life with its way before us lies,
> Christ is the path and Christ the prize.

Some Christians call themselves "soldiers". They are members of the Salvation Army. Their leaders are officers. They wear uniforms, and the battlefield is life. The enemy is not only inside. As well as the selfishness within there are the evils of poverty, prejudice and injustice to overcome in the outside world. Fourteen-year-old Melissa plays in the Salvation Army band: "Sometimes we play in the main shopping areas in town. The money we collect goes to help the poor. Homeless people that come to our centre get hot food and if they need clothes we can help them. They also join in the worship while they are with us."

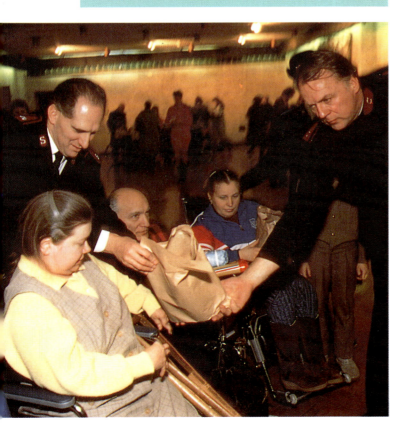

Members of the Salvation Army help in the community to overcome poverty, prejudice and injustice in society.

This is what St Paul had to say about fighting evil:

> So put on God's armour now! Then when the evil day comes, you will be able to resist the enemy's attacks; and after fighting to the end, you will still hold your ground.
>
> So stand ready, with truth as a belt tight round your waist, with righteousness as your breastplate, and as your shoes the readiness to announce the Good News of peace. At all times carry faith as a shield; for with it you will be able to put out all the burning arrows shot by the Evil One. And accept salvation as a helmet, and the word of God as the sword which the Spirit gives you. Do all this in prayer, asking for God's help.
>
> [Ephesians 6:13–18]

 3 What are the weapons St Paul says the Christian should wear? Design a poster of the Christian as a soldier of Christ.

Oscar Romero stands outside his cathedral in El Salvador.

Christians in all Churches are involved in the struggle to establish God's kingdom on earth. For some the fight is very dangerous. Archbishop Oscar Romero lived and worked in El Salvador, in Central America. He was a quiet and gentle man. But he saw the terrible treatment of the poor in his country and he could not keep silent. Romero devoted his life to the cause of justice. In his struggle against poverty he came up against the anger of the rich and powerful. There were many attempts on his life. On 24 March 1980 he was shot dead while he was saying Mass. Archbishop Romero believed that when the powers of evil get too strong, Christians may have to fight.

4 Do you think there are occasions when Christians should be prepared to fight? Find examples of injustice and oppression in the newspapers to help you. Write your answer, giving reasons.

5 Quakers (the Society of Friends) believe that Christians should never take up arms but always use peaceful protest. Find out more about the views of Quakers. How do their views differ from those of Archbishop Romero?

TWENTY-SEVEN

Being Caretakers

Have you ever wondered about where the world came from? In this unit you will try to interpret the meaning of creation stories in the Bible for Christians and consider how they influence the Christian view of the environment.

1 What is your theory about how the world began? Write a summary of your ideas. Share your ideas in class.

2 Read the creation stories in the book of Genesis 1:1–2:4 and 2:5–2:25. Write down three teachings or messages in these stories that you think are important for Christians today. Compare your responses in class.

Christians believe that the universe was created by God. In the first chapters of the Bible there are stories about creation. Some Christians take these stories as word-for-word accounts of what happened. Others look for the meaning behind the story.

In the Garden of Eden human life is seen in harmony with the rest of nature. There are other texts in the Bible that promise a perfect world in the future. Here is the prophet Isaiah's view of a perfect world:

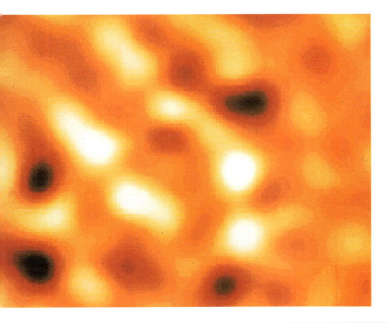

This photo from space may tell us how the Universe looked after the Big Bang.

> " Wolves and sheep will live together in peace,
>   and leopards will lie down with young goats,
> Calves and lion cubs will feed together,
>   and little children will take care of them.
> Cows and bears will eat together,
>   and their calves and cubs will lie down in peace.
> Lions will eat straw as cattle do.
> Even a baby will not be harmed
>   if it plays near a poisonous snake.
> On Zion, God's sacred hill,
>   there will be nothing harmful or evil.
> The land will be as full of knowledge of the Lord
>   as the seas are full of water. "
>
> [Isaiah 11:6–9]

3 Put the meaning of Isaiah's vision in your own words. Say how this perfect future compares with the real world today. Use news cuttings, drawings or pictures to contrast with the picture of Isaiah 11.

4 Write a poem or piece of prose that describes what you think would be the perfect world.

Concern for harmony between the human and the animal kingdoms is not a new trend in the Christian tradition. St Francis is a popular saint. He chose a life in harmony with nature. He saw God's power and presence in the beauty of the world and saw all living creatures as his family. It is said that wild animals knew no fear when they were near him and that he bought lambs to save them from slaughter and took injured animals into his care.

Many Christians today are concerned that humans are not taking care of God's world:

> ❝ The world does not really belong to us. It is not ours to spoil. In the Bible it says that men and women were given the Garden of Eden to look after it and to enjoy its fruits. But we are just destroying the garden and showing no respect for God's creation. ❞
> [Amanda, 16]

> ❝ Christians must have a sense of responsibility for others. We cannot leave the world in a mess for future generations. This is why we must try to protect the environment. ❞
> [Guy, 13]

▶ What do you think that Christians can do to try to save the world they believe that God has given them? Design a paper for church discussion groups using texts from the Bible, pictures and questions for discussion.

5 St Francis was declared the Patron Saint of Ecologists by the Pope. Find out more about St Francis and design a poster to promote the celebration of St Francis's day.

St Francis of Assisi loved all of God's creation. Here he is preaching to the birds.

Monks at Mount Athos meet environmentalists to discuss a logging project.

TWENTY-EIGHT

Facing Death

What can we do in the face of death? What happens after death? In this unit you will look at these questions and learn about some Christian responses.

> **1** Some say that every day we should remember that we will die. In this way we will learn to live. Do you think there is any truth in this argument? Write down your thoughts then share them in class.

> **2** What words and phrases are used to talk about dying to avoid the word "dead"? Write down your answers. Why are there problems in talking about death? Share your ideas in class.

Christians have to look death in the face. At the heart of the Christian faith is the story of the death of a man.

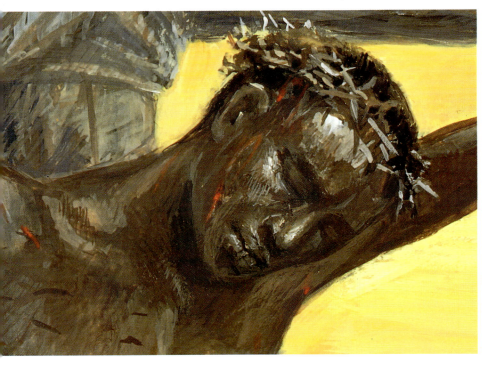

> **3** Brian, aged 17, said: "Jesus taught us to remember that death may come at any moment. This is why we must live each day as if it were our last." How would you live if you were living each day as if it were your last? Would you behave differently towards others? Would you say or do things differently? Would you notice things you take for granted? Describe one day as if lived in this way – write it as a diary entry.

"When I look at Jesus on the cross and think about the way he died it makes me think about what it must be like to die. And I have to remember that I shall die one day."
[Kaye, 14]

In some Christian homes when someone is close to death the family calls the priest or minister. He or she will hear the confession of the person who is dying or just sit with them. Sometimes the dying person is offered Holy Communion. Deborah, who is 15, finds the words of Jesus helpful in coming to terms with the death of someone close: "Jesus said, 'I am the resurrection and the life.' These words are important for Christians, especially when they are facing death or mourning the loss of a loved one. That is why these words are often said at funerals."

A Christian funeral service is usually conducted by a church minister or priest. The minister offers words of comfort for the bereaved. He or she gives thanks for the life that has ended and asks God to receive the spirit of the person who has died.

❝ Before the funeral the body is washed and dressed and laid in a coffin. In our church the coffin is open at the funeral service so that friends and family can pay their respects. ❞
[Linda, 14]

❝ I don't know what will happen exactly on the other side of the grave but I do know that Jesus has been there. ❞
[Thomas, 16]

At a cemetery in Brazil on All Souls' Day Christians burn candles in honour of those who have died.

 4 Read the teaching of St Paul on the Christian hope of resurrection in 1 Corinthians 15:35–58. Write some words of comfort and thanksgiving that a minister might say at a funeral, using these words of St Paul to help you.

 5 Write down the different beliefs that you have met about life after death. Say which of these expresses the Christian belief and say what you believe. Discuss your answers with a friend and share your ideas in class.

Many Christians visit the graves of those who have died. They take flowers or go to spend time in silent thought and prayer. Twelve-year-old Janosh, who is from the Orthodox tradition, said: "In our church we make a boiled wheat pudding on the anniversary of the death of a relative. The wheat is a reminder of the resurrection. Just as wheat grains sprout into new life so the dead will rise again like Christ."

 6 Read Psalm 23. These words are often sung or said at funerals. Why do you think people choose this psalm? Put the psalm into your own words – a modern version if you wish.

59

TWENTY-NINE

Celebrating Life

Everyone loves a celebration. In this unit you will discuss what is worth celebrating and find out about the ways in which Christians celebrate life.

 1. *What do people celebrate? Love? Success? A new home? Make a list of ten things that you think are worth celebrating. Compare your list with a partner. Share your ideas in class.*

 2. *How do people celebrate? What do they do to express their happiness or success? With a partner come up with ten ways to celebrate. Compare your ideas in class.*

Christians believe that the good things in life are given by God and that they should be enjoyed and celebrated. Every Sunday is a celebration for Christians. In the creation story in the Bible (Genesis 1:1–2:4) God sets aside a day of rest, a special day after six days of work. This is why many Christians go to church to give thanks for God's goodness. In some homes Sunday is treated like a festival. The family comes together for a shared meal and the work and worries of the week are put to one side. Sunday is a time to enjoy God's creation. Thirteen-year-old Eve said: "In our church we celebrate God's love with music, with joyful clapping and singing. We make as much noise as we can to express our happiness and praise."

Some Christians celebrate through dance. Ann-Marie said that dancing is important in the worship in her church. "It involves the whole person, body, mind, senses, imagination and emotions. You can really express your feelings in dance."

These young Christians are singing and dancing at Spring Harvest, at Weston-Super-Mare in 1996.

Christians believe that the resurrection of Christ showed that death is not the end. They claim there is no longer any need to live in fear of death. Life can be free of fear and lived to the full. The whole of life can become a celebration.

❝ The Bible says God can create "a new heaven and a new earth". We can experience this new existence in our own lives. We do not have to live our lives cramped by guilt, shame and fear of death. We can become new people living life to the full. ❞
[Marsha, 14]

❝ Christians celebrate life in many ways. Working, sharing food, teaching, learning, travelling, meeting new people, being with loved ones, enjoying nature, listening to music, serving others – these can all become acts of celebration. ❞
[David, 23]

3 Find out about the way Christians celebrate some of the lesser festivals of the Christian year such as Harvest Thanksgiving, All Saints' Day, Shrove Tuesday, Ascension Day.

4 In our culture we have lost many of the feast days and celebrations that people enjoyed in the past. Do you think we need new opportunities for celebration? If you were to introduce a new festival to our calendar what would it celebrate? Discuss your ideas in class.

5 If there were to be an international day for the celebration of life – how should it be celebrated? What activities would have to stop for the day? What activities would be an appropriate expression for the celebration of life? Describe your ideas for the celebration in an advertisement.

This mural, showing the Ascension, was painted in Cyprus 800 years ago. Christians believe that Christ ascended into heaven. Now they must carry out his work and celebrate his life on earth.

GLOSSARY

Advent "Coming", a time of preparation leading up to the "coming" of Christ at Christmas, the beginning of the Church year

Anglican churches A group of churches which includes the Church of England

Apostle One of the twelve disciples sent to preach the gospel

Baptism Religious ceremony when a person is immersed in or sprinkled with water. In Christianity it shows a person has become a member of the Christian Church

Baptist Church Free church that began in the 17th century; its members reject the practice of infant baptism

Believers' Baptism Baptism of people who are old enough to understand the meaning of the event

Bible The Holy Scriptures of the Christian faith

Christening Infant baptism

Christian A follower of Christ

Church The whole community of Christians; the building in which Christians worship; a particular group of Christians

Confession Owning up to wrong-doing and asking for forgiveness

Confirmation A religious ceremony expressing the intention to hold firm to the faith

Disciple A follower of Jesus

Easter The main Christian festival (in March or April) which celebrates the resurrection of Jesus

Eucharist Service of thanksgiving in which bread and wine are shared, when worshippers remember the last supper

Evangelist Someone who preaches the Gospel

Good Friday Christian day of mourning marking the death of Christ on the cross

Gospel "Good news". The preaching of Jesus; also the accounts of his life by Matthew, Mark, Luke and John

Holy Communion See Eucharist

Holy Spirit The third person of the Trinity, the power and presence of God at work in the Church and its members

Holy Week When Christians remember the last week in the life of Jesus before his death on the cross

Icon Religious picture sometimes used in prayer or worship, especially in the Orthodox tradition

Incarnation The belief that God took human form in Jesus

Intercession Prayer that asks for help

Last Supper The last meal Jesus ate with his friends

Lent Forty days leading up to Easter, a time of preparation and repentance

Liturgy Orthodox service of Eucharist

Mass See Eucharist

Methodist Church Church that began with an 18th-century movement to tell people about Jesus

New Testament Collection of twenty-seven books that form the second part of the Christian Bible. The first four books are the Gospels

Old Testament Collection of thirty-nine books that form the first part of the Christian Bible

Orthodox Church that separated from the Catholic tradition in 1054; often refers to members of the Russian and Greek traditions

Pentecost The day Christians remember the coming of the Holy Spirit

Pentecostal Church that emphasises the power of the Holy Spirit in its worship

Pilgrimage A religious journey, a journey of faith

Protestant Churches that separated from the Roman Catholic Church beginning in the 16th century

Quakers See Society of Friends

Repentance Expressing sorrow and shame for wrongdoing and asking for the chance to try again

Resurrection The event of Christ rising from the dead; the event of believers rising from the dead

Roman Catholic Church that looks to the Pope as its head

Sacrament An outward sign of an inward blessing, e.g. marriage, confirmation, Eucharist

Sin Wrongdoing, sense of being separated from God

Society of Friends A group of Christians also called Quakers, begun in the 17th century

Trinity God as Father, Son and Holy Spirit, three in one

Answer to Question 4 on page 5. They are all Christians. Pictures show African worshippers, an Indian Roman Catholic, a drive-in church in America, a Methodist church, an Orthodox service, and a Pentecostal service.

INDEX

Advent 30, 31
Anglican 7, 38, 39, 54
Apostles 44
Ash Wednesday 40

Baptism 36, 37, 38
Baptist Church 7
Bible 7, 10, 12, 56, 60
Bishop 7, 38
Breaking Bread *see* Eucharist

Christening 36
Christmas 30, 32, 33
Church/churches 6, 7, 10, 18, 36, 38, 51
Confirmation 38, 39
Convent 53

Disciples 8, 9, 13, 28

Easter 42, 43
Eucharist 26, 27, 38, 39, 42, 58
Evangelist 10, 11

God 14
Good Friday 41
Gospel 12, 13, 23

Holy Communion *see* Eucharist
Holy Liturgy 26, 27
Holy Spirit 15, 38, 44, 45
Hymn 22

Icon 17, 33, 44, 46
Incarnation 33
Intercession 20, 21

John the Baptist 31

Last Supper 26
Lent 40, 41
Lord's Supper *see* Eucharist

Mass *see* Eucharist
Methodist Church 50
Monastery 53

New Testament 12

Old Testament 12, 31
Orthodox Church 7, 13, 18, 33, 43, 46

Palestine 8
Pentecost 44
Pentecostal Church 28, 45
Pilgrimage 48
Prayer 18, 19, 20, 21, 45, 46
Protestant Church 7

Quaker *see* Society of Friends

Repentance 34, 36, 40
Resurrection 42, 43, 58, 61
Roman Catholic Church 6, 46, 38
Rosary 19

Sacraments 27
Saints 46, 47, 57
Salvation Army Church 24, 54
Sermon 10
Sin 34, 35, 38
Society of Friends 10, 11, 25, 51, 55
Synagogue 18

Trinity 15

ACKNOWLEDGEMENTS

The author and publishers would like to thank the following for permission to reproduce photographs:

Andes Press Agency/Carlos Rayes Marizo: pp 5 (middle right), 23 (top), 24, 28, 36 (left), 37, 38, 42, 45, 50; Andes Press Agency/Oleg Svyatoslansky: p 43 (bottom); Bridgeman Art Library/State Russian Museum, St Petersburg: p 33; Bridgeman Art Library, London/Fitzwilliam Museum, University of Cambridge: p 47; Bridgeman Art Library, London/Giraudon : p 57 (top); Bridgeman Art Library, London/Bibliotheque Nationale, Rouen: p 44 ; Christian Aid/Nick Davies: p 21; CIRCA Photo Library/ICOREC: pp 4 (left), 12, 13, 26, 36 (right), 57 (bottom); CIRCA Photo Library/ICOREC/Mike Edwards: p 39; CIRCA Photo Library/ICOREC/John Fryer: p 40; CIRCA Photo Library/ICOREC/John Smith: pp 18 (top), 19, 27; Sally and Richard Greenhill: pp 29, 30; Sonia Halliday Photographs: p 61; Sonia Halliday Photographs/Laura Lushington: p 15; Peter Hammer Verlag: p 9; The Hutchison Library/ Macintyre: p 18 (bottom); Magnum/Ian Berry: p 11 (top middle); Magnum/P J Griffiths: p 49; Magnum/ Susan Heiselas: p 55; Magnum/Fred Mayer: p 48; Network Photographers Ltd/Gideon Mendell: p 16; Panos Pictures: p 6 (right); Panos Pictures/Jeremy Hartley: p 5 (left); Panos Pictures/Roderick Johnson: p 4 (right); Panos Pictures/Eric Millar: p 43; Pictor: p 22; Popperfoto: p 23 (bottom); Rex Features/Sipa Press: p 54; Morris Rowlandson/Evangelical Association Global Mission: p 11 (top left); The Salvation Army: pp 6 (left), 25; Scala: pp 17 (left), 35; The Science Photo Library: p 56; The Library Committee of Britain Yearly Meeting of the Religious Society of Friends: pp 11 (top right), 51; South American Pictures/Robert Francis: p 46; South American Pictures/Tony Morrison: pp 32, 59; Spring Harvest: pps 14, 60; Imogen Stuart R.H.A./Ballintubber Abbey Trust: p 41; Times Newspapers/Chris Harris: p 34; Topham Picturepoint: p 5 (bottom and top right); Tropix: p 53; Vie de Jesus Mafa: pp 11 (bottom), 17 (right), 47 (left), 58; Yes Magazine/Philippa Smethurst (Church Mission Society): p 20; Yes Magazine/Jeremy Thompson (Church Mission Society): p 31.

Cover Photo: Panos/ Eric Millar

Artwork was provided by:
Tony Morris pp 8, 53; Oxford Illustrators pp 7, 32; Oxprint pp 14, 34, 52.

OXFORD
UNIVERSITY PRESS

Great Clarendon Street, Oxford OX2 6DP
Oxford Press is a department of the University of Oxford. It furthers the University's objective of excellence in research, scholarship, and education by publishing worldwide in

Oxford New York

Auckland Cape Town Dar es Salaam Hong Kong Karachi Kuala Lumpur Madrid Melbourne Mexico City Nairobi New Delhi Shanghai Taipei Toronto

With offices in

Argentina Austria Brazil Chile Czech Republic France Greece Guatemala Hungary Italy Japan Poland Portugal Singapore South Korea Switzerland Thailand Turkey Ukraine Vietnam

Oxford is a registered trade mark of Oxford University Press in the UK and in certain other countries

© Oxford University Press

The moral rights of the author have been asserted

First published 1997

All rights reserved. No part of this publication may be reproduced, stored in a retrieval system, or transmitted, in any form or by any means, without prior permission of Oxford University Press. Within the UK, exceptions are allowed in respect of any fair dealing for the purpose of research or private study, or criticism or review, as permitted under the Copyright, Designs and Patents Act 1988, or in the case of reprographic reproduction in accordance with the terms of the licences issued by the Copyright Licensing Agency. Enquiries concerning reproduction outside these terms and in other countries should be sent to the Rights Department, Oxford University Press, at the address above.

This book is sold subject to the condition that it shall not, by way of trade or otherwise, be lent, re-sold, hired or otherwise circulated, without the publisher's prior consent in any form of binding or cover other than that in which it is published and without a similar condition including this condition being imposed on the subsequent purchaser.

British Library Cataloguing in Publication Data available

ISBN 13 9780199172405

ISBN 0 19 917240 4

10 9 8 7

Printed in Singapore by KHL Printing Co Pte Ltd